MW01701466

THE LESSONS I HAVE LEARNED FROM EXILE

"I don't know how, I don't know when, but I know He will."
- Justin Andrew Duncan

Recognizing Some Godly Principles That Can Help You

Conquer Your Life's Struggles

By

Turning Your Pain into a Path to Success

By
Justin Andrew Duncan

Paperback ISBN: 978-1-63901-243-5

First Printing edition 2021.

Fiorella Cintron Editor
fiorella.cintron@gmail.com

To my wonderful wife Elina without whose love and support, this book would have not been possible.

I would also like to thank Dorian Leslie for walking every step of this journey with me. My daughter Ariel and two sons Christian & Adin, for being my inspiration. My dearest friends, Marcel McNeil, George and Maryann Flores, Valerie Fullilove, Bernard Blunt, Sister Powell, Pat Malvo, and the entire Spirit and Truth Center for Worship family.

All scriptures are taken from the King James Version of the Bible unless otherwise stated.

CONTENTS

The Lessons I Have Learned from Exile

Introduction 1

Chapter One: Double Lost 3

Chapter Two: God gave me what I needed, not what I wanted 9

Chapter Three: The Lord still speaks to us through dreams 16

Chapter Four: Remember me 25

Chapter Five: My favorite Bible verse 31

Chapter Six: Commitment 37

Chapter Seven: You will be restored 43

Chapter Eight: The cup of water 49

Chapter Nine: The 2020 Christmas Miracle, one of many 59

Chapter Ten: A great way to overcome sin and addictions 70

Chapter Eleven: A Gift 76

Chapter Twelve: Give sacrificially (Love) 85

INTRODUCTION

I have known all my life that I have been called to the ministry. No matter how often I ran from the responsibility, or thought by some sin or mistake that God had disqualified me. I can now clearly see that every misstep has been used by the Lord to give me an experience that serves me well as I endeavour to fulfill my destiny. This book is not based on a true story. This book is a true story. As you read further, I pray that you will gain valuable insights into practical lifestyle changes that will help you fulfill your destiny.

CHAPTER ONE: DOUBLE LOST

It was 2012. My youngest brother, Dorian Leslie, came to my house, while I was lying in bed during the day. I was suffering from a deep paralyzing and painful depression. He summed up my current state in life with five short simple words. He said, "Justin, you are double lost!"

Double lost? What's that? He proceeded to explain it to me as I frowned while scrutinizing the real meaning of those powerful words. He said, "When you're lost, you know it. For example: you stop at the gas station or convenience store, or you stop someone on the street and ask for directions." He continued, "You're so lost that you don't know that you're lost; you never stop and ask for directions... You just keep on going the wrong way. You think that you are on the right path, not realizing that you are speeding along the wrong direction. You continue to get yourself further and further from your destination. As you travel on your journey, you're not only hurting yourself, but you are hurting all of the people connected to you."

Those few words caused me to do something I had never really done in my life; it caused me to stop and look at myself... I mean a long, hard look as if I were looking into a mirror that would enable me to look into my soul. But this mirror looked into my motivations, my actions, and my character.

For days at a time, I was afraid to look at myself that deeply and analyze the decisions that I had made in life because I was afraid of what I might see. But my life was in such distress, I was in such a dark place... My marriage was all but over; my kids didn't have respect for me; and after losing my dream job, I couldn't find a job that matched my experience or provide enough to feed my family. I was depressed and in bed most of the time. When I spoke to people, the things that came out of my mouth came from a depleted place. I was in physical and emotional pain, so, I didn't speak to people the right way. I had no wisdom and I felt like my relationship with the Lord was hanging on by a thread; and that small thread was the red cord of his grace.

> *My marriage was all but over; my kids didn't have respect for me; and after losing my dream job, I couldn't find a job that matched my experience or provide enough to my family. I was depressed and in bed most of the time.*

I was not able to drive a car because my driver's license was suspended. It was suspended because I couldn't afford car insurance and like a fool, I drove around without car insurance. Of course, the police stopped me. I had thousands of dollars in driver's license related fines and surcharges that were due. I was in all types of financial debt and couldn't see a solution to any of my problems; but, deep inside, I still believed that God created me for more than this. I faithfully believed that the gifts he had given me were an indication that he created me for something greater.

Let's fast forward. My ex-wife and I had agreed to get a divorce. For the next 5 years, I was living in one room, yes, one room that had two closets and a window. I rented, from an elderly widow, an upper room on the third floor of her house for $140 per week. I had to share a bathroom with another gentleman who rented a room down the hall. After leaving Home Depot as Garden Department Supervisor, I was working for Amazon as a packer during the overnight shift. Now, if you're not familiar with that job, it goes like this: I'm standing on my feet all night except for three breaks, which I could not take at my leisure. They are all scheduled. The first one was a half hour break for lunch and the other two were 15-minute breaks; and we all had to take them together. Afterwards, I would have to go back and pack items in boxes as quickly as possible to maintain a certain rate in order to keep from getting fired.

I was earning $15 an hour. Much of what I took home went towards support payments for my youngest son. These payments were not court ordered. My ex-wife and I agreed that I would give $600 a month, and so I consistently did this to help support my youngest son.

During this time, my commitment to the Lord increased. Although I worked Thursday through Saturday 5:00 PM to 5:30 AM and had to take the bus to and from work, I still managed to get around two hours of sleep and get to service on time every Sunday morning at 10:00 AM. At that time, I was the church musician and an occasional preacher, and received $100.00 per Sunday as the church musician. Up until that point it was five years of separation from my family. I was praying that the Lord would bring my ex-wife and my kids back together, but the damage was too severe... I caused too much damage. Trust was broken and it was not going to be restored at that time. With a broken marriage, broken family, I was trying to survive on low pay. It seemed like the only thing I had in my life that was getting better was my relationship with God. It's funny how you trust God when your back is against the wall and there is not enough space to breathe or move; all hope seems to be lost and the only safe space is that place where you barely hear that *faint, still, small* voice.

> *It's funny how you trust God when your back is against the wall and there is not enough space to breathe or move; all hope seems to be lost and the only safe space is that place where you barely hear that faint, still, small voice.*

While I was going through this time of vast emptiness, brokenness, and separation from family, I would spend time praying and fasting. God would reveal things to me that would let me know I was born for such a time as this. I continued my practice of fasting every Wednesday. The reason why I fast on that specific day is because I believe in giving God my first fruits, which is "Christian-ease" or "Christian cultural speak" for giving God the first or the best parts of what I have received. I was born on June 9th, 1965. It was on a Wednesday. I see Wednesday as the beginning of my week, and so I fast every Wednesday to give God the first day of my week or the "First Fruits" of my week. With all of the chaos and turmoil that surrounded me, I didn't know it, but it was the perfect time for God to change my character, to humble me, to do what only he could do in order to transform me.

Take away: When you're in trouble, increase your commitment to the Lord. Schedule a set time to pray each day, add fasting to your lifestyle, and find a place like a church or Christ centered charitable organization where you can serve people in his name. Finally, I know it sounds hard when things are so tight and you have such little money, but return to the Lord a tithe, which means a 10% of your gross income and watch God be faithful to his word. As seen in the Bible, the Lord once said,

> *...Prove me now herewith, saith the Lord of hosts, if I will not open you the windows of heaven, and pour you out a blessing that shall not be room enough to receive it. And I will rebuke the devour for your sakes (King James Version Bible, Mal. 3.10-11).*

CHAPTER TWO: GOD GAVE ME WHAT I NEEDED, NOT WHAT I WANTED

For the five plus years of separation from my family I prayed that the Lord would reunite us. I would find time each day to pray that the Lord would fix the mistakes that I had made in the past and enable me to do some good deeds to show my family that I had changed. I wish I could tell you that a miracle took place, and everything worked out just the way I had prayed, but sometimes in life things don't happen the way we want them to happen. There is a consequence to sin and although the Lord forgives us, and even if the injured party forgives us, there is still pain. There is also a lack of trust that takes a long time, sometimes a lifetime to be resolved; and in some cases, like mine, when you have blown your last opportunity... the Lord closes the door, but He also opens a window.

It was a couple of days before Thanksgiving, 2018. I was walking back to my upper room. I wish I could say it was a one room apartment, but it was one room in Irvington, New Jersey. Heartbroken that things didn't work out with my family, I could literally feel the pain in my chest, my heart beating with heavy breathing as if I was having a panic attack. I came to the realization that I would never have the family unit, nice and neatly packaged, just like I had prayed for. After a while, I came to the realization that God would have to work something else out in my life as well as in my family's life.

It was the Saturday after Thanksgiving. I had just finished the overnight shift and got home at around 7:00 AM Sunday morning. I slept until around 9:00 AM, so, with two hours of sleep I was very tired, but I had made a commitment to the Lord to be at church every Sunday. I strongly believed back then, and I do believe now, that one of the keys to success in life is having a commitment. That means that you stick with it even when you don't feel like it; you stick with it when it is not easy; you stick with it when you're discouraged; you stick with it when you receive no praise or no money.

> *I strongly believed back then, and I do believe now, that one of the keys to success in life is having a commitment.*

With two hours of sleep, I went to service; however, because it was the holiday season at Amazon, I was called in to do a mandatory overtime overnight shift. So, I left the Church, got on the bus, and headed down to Amazon to work another overnight shift. I really thought about calling out sick, but I said to myself, "I made a commitment to work these extra overnight shifts and I know the Lord wants me to be more committed in my life."

My lack of commitment was one of the main reasons my marriage failed. There were times in the past when I had a lack of commitment. I desperately wanted to change that character flaw in my life. Consciously, I chose things to be committed to. Believing that my commitment, with the Lord's help, would change things in my life.

With two hours of sleep, I got over to Amazon and clocked in at 5:00 PM. I walked up to my station where I was working an induction machine, sending what we called "smart packs". Those are the blue and white plastic packages you receive from Amazon. It was my job to manually feed these packages through the induction machines while checking the packages for errors at the same time. Because this was an extra shift for me and not my usual day to work, I followed the lead of the people who normally work that shift and... there she was. Her name is Elina. As we got ready to work, we all introduced ourselves to each other and Elina introduced herself to me.

While the others were manually feeding the packages through the machines, I was assigned to the computer as the problem solver; the one who would receive the packages that had problems and work the computer to correct the errors. There was something about Elina that really caught my eye. She is stunning with beautiful light-colored skin, wonderful long hair, pretty face, in great shape, and those breathtaking green eyes... But that's not what caught my attention at first sight because at that time in my life I was not looking for anyone. I felt that I was not worthy to be entrusted to take care of another woman. I sensed that she had so much going for her with her natural beauty and the fact that she was bilingual. Spanish is her native language, but her English is excellent. It seemed to me that she has so much God given favor, but there was sadness in her eyes, and it made me so curious. I needed to know why this woman would have such sadness in her eyes and seem to be suffering from low self-esteem?

I told her that I had seen many beautiful women from all around the world because of my previous life. I was a sales manager and traveled to many states; I also had the opportunity to travel to other countries, and compared to all of those women that I had seen, I thought she was exceptionally beautiful, but she didn't see it herself. It was as if she didn't see herself in that light. Even now, she is still extremely modest. In my spirit, I knew someone did something to her and I had an overwhelming desire to encourage her and help her see who she really was. I asked her for her phone number and called her the next day, not knowing if she would answer my phone call. To my surprise, she did. We worked different shifts, so we were never able to see each other for months. God knew in his infinite wisdom that it was the best thing for us.

For months, our conversations were text messages back-and-forth. We laughed uncontrollably through our text messages. You would think there was no way for us to survive on such little sleep because we spent so much time texting each other, but for some reason, we were able to go to work and function. We continued our textathons after one of us got home from our shift. It became my mission in life to encourage her and help her see the person that God created her to be. After months of texting, we started speaking on the phone and little by little I started to fall in love. We even got to the point where we could do video chats over the phone and the feelings became mutual. Meeting this special person made my depression fade away. What if I had not gone into work that day? What if I had decided I was too tired? I would have missed out on this incredible gift that the Lord has given to me.

> *After months of texting, we started speaking on the phone and little by little I started to fall in love.*

Months after my divorce came through, on January 31st, 2020, Elina became my wife. This was not what I had prayed for during the five years of separation. I never thought that my life would have gone in this direction. I realize that so many people are praying for a partner; I never prayed for Elina. However, I did pray to be closer to the Lord; I did pray to be in the center of his will; I did pray for the Lord to change me and make me a better person. During my years of separation, I never once did anything inappropriate with a woman and I have never in my life even considered doing anything inappropriate with a man. I've never been wired that way. I made a commitment to the Lord and I believe he honored that commitment with the perfect partner for me.

During our times of courtship, we could not meet physically. We texted and spoke to each other over the phone for months. It is still amazing to me to see how we were able to send text messages and it was like we were both looking at a video screen, seeing the same thing at the same time, and laughing at the same images in our minds. I believe that was the foundation for a strong relationship; all the time that we spent getting to know each other without any physical contact. The foundation of our relationship was never sexual compatibility. It has always been, and I believe it always will be, our ability to communicate, being able to put oneself in the other person's shoes, to share the difficult and the trivial things, to find time to laugh, to find time to learn, to make time to dance, to sing, and most of all, we take time to pray and worship the Lord together.

During our times of courtship, we could not meet physically. We texted and spoke to each other over the phone for months.

We both tried our best to put the other person first and respect our differences. Elina was raised to be a devout Catholic. I was raised to be an ardent Pentecostal. We have many differences, but our love and respect for each other, which was derived from learning from our past relationships, has helped us have a smooth transition into re-marriage. All of the physical benefits are just icing on the cake.

Take away: Instead of spending much of your life on finding that new wife or that new husband, chase the Lord by looking to fulfill the gifts and talents that He has given you through service to him. It is when you replace "me time" with "knee time", and when you spend your time focusing on pleasing the Lord that He will send you that perfect person. The person who will help you accomplish God's purpose in your life. The Bible says, "Commit thy way unto the Lord; trust also in him; and he shall bring it to pass" (Psalm. 37.5).

CHAPTER THREE: THE LORD STILL SPEAKS TO US THROUGH DREAMS

In the Bible the Lord says that "He changes not" (Mal. 3.6). The same God that spoke to Joseph through dreams, Daniel through visions, and spoke to Peter in a vision on the rooftop, speaks to us through our dreams today. No, not every dream is a spiritual dream from God... absolutely not. And even if it is a dream from God, we must be sure that the Lord wants us to share it. Some thoughts are to be kept like Mary, the mother of Jesus. The Bible says that she pondered these things in her heart (Luk. 2.19).

I have noticed that throughout my life, the closer I am to the Lord, and the more consistently I am following his words, the more frequent the Lord speaks to me through my dreams. I believe that if you want the Lord to speak to you through your dreams, it's time to step up your commitment to him and he will warn you of the plans of the enemy, or he show you a way of escape, or even share something with you that will affect future decisions and steer you in the direction where He wants you to go.

I believe there are two types of *dreamers* or *seers* as the Bible used to call them. One type of dreamer is the person who steps up their commitment to the Lord. They begin to see that God interacts with them more frequently through their dream life. The other type of dreamer is the person who is naturally gifted to see dreams and visions. My wife Elina is the latter. Very often, the Lord speaks to her through her dreams. One night she dreamt that I was pulling her by the hand, leading her out of the job that she was in at Amazon, and months later, God used that dream to represent how she would finally be able to leave that job. During this time, I was driving for Uber and Lyft trying to make a living, but it wasn't going so well. It seems like whatever little money I made went towards gas and tolls. Leaving me extremely tired and financially frustrated.

> *They begin to see that God interacts with them more frequently through their dream life.*

Elina was extremely unhappy working for Amazon. As I would drive her to work each day at around 4 o'clock, when we were about to get onto Route one in Edison New Jersey, she would just start crying... She was so unhappy with how she was treated and the hard work that she had to do. She seemed caught between a rock and a hard place because I wasn't really bringing in any money from all of the driving that I was doing, and we needed income to survive. After the Christmas break, Amazon offered the employees a package of $1,000 for every year of service based on the condition that you can never work for Amazon again. We prayed and prayed and asked the Lord what we should do. Should Elina leave or stay? She was so miserable; I couldn't see how it would be God's will for her to stay, but I also was aware that the income was very much needed. That is when we remembered Elina's dream. She dreamt that while in Amazon, I was leading her by the hand pulling her out. We took a huge leap of faith and took the package trusting that the Lord would help us with our next step.

> *We prayed and prayed and asked the Lord what we should do.*

We were both around 54 years of age at that time and as many of you know, it is not easy finding a job at that age. Although Elina had a bachelor's degree in chemistry, no chemistry doors opened. Then came the COVID-19 pandemic. Elina interviewed with a company and we were all sure that she would get the job. However, when the pandemic hit, they could not hire anyone. The state of New Jersey was in lockdown. I was also furloughed from a job that I had at a clothing store as a salesperson.

We needed the Lord to help us with unemployment insurance. I filled out the online documentation and I was waiting to get an answer. Because Elina left Amazon, she felt that she was not entitled to receive unemployment insurance and so she did not file. She also really didn't want me to file for her because she thought it would be a waste of time, but I believe the Lord shared with me that she should file. Because of the pandemic, she was not able to get in with the company that she left Amazon for. So, with her permission, I filed for her.

With much prayer, we had to go through seven weeks of not knowing if we were going to receive money from New Jersey's unemployment insurance. During those seven weeks, we continued to give the Lord an offering every week out of the savings from which we were living. We had already tithed off the money in our savings account, but we needed the Lord to act on our behalf, so we started to give him offerings. I got up every morning at 6:00 AM and prayed even to the point where the landlord called me up and asked me if I could tone it down in the mornings because he was not able to get all the sleep he was looking to get. And of course, the stress was building, and fear was trying to take hold.

When it got to the seventh week, I started to prophesy that the Lord was going to give us the money next week. As Elina and I were sitting in our home office trying to figure out our next steps, I heared the Lord saying, "It's about relationships." Then the senators of New Jersey came to mind and I called their offices. All I received was an answering machine from both Senator Melendez' office and Senator Booker's office. So, I thought, "Who else could I call?" That is when I searched on Google for a local Congressperson. Google said it was Donald Payne Jr. So, I decided to call his office and to my surprise, a young lady answered the phone saying, "Donald Payne Junior's office, how can I help you?" I explained our situation; that we had filed for unemployment insurance and we have been waiting for seven weeks with no answer. She said that this was a state matter, and they usually handle only federal matters; however, they had received so many calls regarding the same matter. She said that if we signed a waiver giving them permission to act on our behalf, they would try to help us. She emailed over the waiver, we signed it, scanned it, and emailed it back. Within three business days of doing that, I received an email from the New Jersey Department of Labor telling me that the money that we needed was on the way.

One week later, Elina received an email asking her to fill out some additional information and was told that her money was on the way. After seven long weeks of not having any income, God provided both of us with seven weeks of unemployment insurance at one time, helping us to stay afloat. It was the dream that God gave Elina that gave us the confidence to step out in faith and leave the security of a consistent paycheck. Now we are free to do the things that God has called us to do.

In the beginning of this chapter, I had mentioned two types of dreamers. I am the latter of the two. I have to fast and pray my way into God given messages that are revealed through dreams and visions. On October 3rd, 2019, I had one of those dreams. I dreamt that I was at Home Depot walking through the contractor's parking area towards the building materials entrance. I saw a tall elderly Africian-American gentleman who seemed to be in excellent health, loading wood into the back of a purple Dodge Durango SUV. A second later, I found myself inside a church. I knew that I needed to speak with the Pastor.

I approached two men at the entrance of a room and asked, “Are one of you the Pastor?”

They said, “No, he’s down the hall.”

When I got to the office, sitting in the chair behind a desk was the man that I saw loading wood into his purple vehicle.

He looked up at me and said, “So, you’re the guy!” And he handed me a silver key.

I awoke from the dream trying to figure out the interpretation of the dream. I put on my theological hat and thought, "Silver?" Perhaps God is redeeming me for silver in the bible represents redemption. Maybe the Lord is going to give me some sort of wisdom, some insight that will unlock a door? I knew the Lord wanted me to be a Pastor, but I couldn't see how it could happen. I had no money, and I didn't have a congregation. Even if people wanted to follow me as I follow Christ, I didn't have a church building to have services. A dear friend, Valerie, knew that I was in need of a church. So, she set up an appointment with a Pastor. I had no idea of what could be arranged because I had no money and no congregation. But in faith, I asked Elina to join me to meet with this Pastor.

On the way to the church in Millburn, N.J., I shared with Elina that I had envisioned fellowshipping in a little white church, for I had seen it in Union, N.J. and that image kept coming back to me. To our surprise, when we drove up the church it was a little white church on Church Street in Millburn, N.J. We noticed the number of the building, it is 54-56. That number stood out to us because at the time of this meeting we were both 54 years old. We understand that in Hebrew words are read from right to left. So, the 56 becomes 65. That was significant because we were both born in the year 1965. It was as if the Spirit of the living God was clearly confirming that we were on the right path.

At this time, Pastor Eyesha Marable of the Mount Zion African Methodist Episcopal Church of Millburn, N.J. arrived. She is a petite woman with a beautiful speaking voice. She greeted us as she opened the door. She said, "Welcome, this is your new home." As if an angel was speaking through her, reassuring us that everything had already been worked out.

I had two prime concerns. Number one: The price of the rent and Number two: The time that we would be allowed to have service. Pastor Eyesha allowed us to rent at a grace of God price, of which I am so grateful. Then she was willing to move her service to later in the day so we could start our service at 9 AM on Sundays. Who does that? I don't know of any Pastor that would move their service to accommodate someone that they just met. This is God! After our meeting, she put in my hand a silver key. The Lord Jesus has the greatest sense of humor I've ever experienced. Later on in the week as I contemplated the dream, His sense of humor came through. Here I am asking God, "Was the silver key a symbol of redemption? Or a promise of supernatural understanding?" and the Lord answers, "I gave you a silver in the dream so you could open up the church". With that I laughed and gave him the praise for knowing how to speak to me in a way that I would always remember.

Take away: God often moves through relationships. He will use people that you know or put you in touch with people who are connected to the one that will give you what you need. If the Lord gives you a word through a dream and you have confirmed that it is the Lord, stand on it for he will surely bring it to pass. The Bible says, “Yea, I have spoken it, I will also bring it to pass; I have purposed it, I will also do it" (Isa. 46.11).

CHAPTER FOUR: REMEMBER ME

There are so many ways to tell that Jesus is God. We can tell by the great miracles that he performed; we can tell by the great words that he spoke. Words that changed the lives of those who listened to him, whether it be in his day or today. However, one of the ways that I can tell that Jesus is God, is in the way that he repeated what the Father did, but he did it in his own unique way. One example of that is the way he taught us to remember him. Our Holy Father taught us to remember him when he spoke to the children of Israel. God proclaimed to the children of Israel that they are to keep the feasts of the Lord. Side note: These are not the Jewish feast days; these are the feast days of the Lord. Meaning that these feast days are not only for the Jews to observe.

When Christ returns to earth for the second time and establishes his earthly kingdom, all of mankind will be observing the feast days of the Lord. In the book of Leviticus and Deuteronomy, he detailed seven feasts: Passover, Unleavened Bread, First

Fruits, Pentecost, Trumpets, Atonement & Feast of Tabernacles. Each feast has a specific meaning to Jews and additional meanings to Christians. But what is common to both Christian and Jews is that the Father God used food as a way to remember him. Each old testament feast had certain foods that had to be eaten at certain times. Foods that are bitter to remind us of the suffering that the children of Israel endured; foods that are sweet to remind them of the victory that was theirs when they entered the promised land. Mankind has followed this tradition since that time. We use food to celebrate a birth, to remember a death, to celebrate a promotion or a graduation, a wedding, a Bar Mitzvah, a Sweet 16 Party or a Quinceañera. Whenever we have an event of significance, we usually tie it to food.

One day while I was alone in my room, God revealed to me why he tied food to the seven feasts of the Lord. He did it because our Holy Father wants us to remember him, and our five senses help us remember things.

> *One day while I was alone in my room, God revealed to me why he tied food to the seven feasts of the Lord.*

I recall very clearly when I was about 12 years old, I walked into my parents' bedroom, looked on the dressing table facing the big mirror, and noticed that my father had all the colognes that he would like to wear lined up on the dresser. He had them lined up by the years in which he wore them. I do not remember which came out when, but the order went something like this: Old Spice, Bruit, Stetson & English Leather. I don't know what possessed me to open each bottle and smell them, but I did. When I inhaled each fragrance, it took me back to the decade when my father used to wear that cologne. Old Spice took me back to the 1960s, the decade in which I was born. I specifically remember the house where we lived in England and it brought back long repressed memories. Images that started to flood my mind with memories that I had of those days when I must have been anywhere from 3 to 8 years old. I remembered real Coca-Cola. Not the drink they serve now, but the flavor that's locked up somewhere in a secret vault in Atlanta, Georgia. I took a whiff of the Brute cologne and took me back to the days of the 1970s. A flood of mental images started to pour in, like Joe Namath in stockings. I'll leave that there. It was like what we would call in today's vernacular, a download of information.

I was able to remember where I lived, and the experiences I had during those years. Other fragrances landed me squarely into the 80's, when we used to listen to music by Stevie Wonder, the Police, Michael Jackson, Amy Grant, Matthew Ward and the Second Chapter of Acts, Andre Crouch, and Tremaine Hawkins, just to name a few.

God uses our five senses to help us remember. However, the only way that we can engage our sense of taste is through food. So, the Father God attached each of the seven feasts to specific meals. Each meal has different tastes, different textures, different smells that are accompanied with different sounds and different visual images. When mankind gathers, we have a visual and auditory experience. We may even tie in our sense of touch and smell; however, we can never truly tie in our sense of taste unless food or drink is part of the event. This is the best way to engage all our senses to help us better remember the experience. So, as the Father God did, so did the Son of God, because Jesus is God.

The Lord Jesus did not give us seven different feasts to remember him by. He only gave us one feast. Some of us call it the Eucharist; some of us call it Communion; others call it the Lord's Supper. This feast involves taking emblems that represent the body and the blood of the Lord Jesus Christ. We take a moment to reflect and ask the Lord to forgive us of our sins. We pray to be washed and cleansed of our sins and then we partake of the meal. The emblems help us to remember the Lord Jesus Christ and his death until he comes again. We who partake of this feast gain spiritual strength, physical healing, and emotional and logical clarity as a benefit to taking part in this feast of the Lord, Jesus Christ. Our Lord wants us to remember him. And so, like the father, he ties food to this event.

We have the visual experience of seeing the bread, which resembles the body of Christ. It looks like matzah or wafers. These types of bread have stripes, which reminds us of the whipping that Jesus Christ took before the cross. The bread is flat with no yeast and is bland tasting. Again, reminding us that Jesus Christ's road, that led to our redemption, was not always filled with pleasure. The wine or grape juice has the color of blood, reminding us of the amount of blood that Jesus shed for us; not only on the cross, but before his crucifixion when he was whipped, scourged for our iniquities and for our healing. The grapes are crushed to produce the wine; so was Jesus crushed physically, emotionally, and in spirit to produce our salvation. The smell of the bread and the grape juice reminds us of the smell of blood that Jesus shed as a sacrifice for us. Just like in the old testament where blood was shed for the atonement of Israel's sins; so was the blood of Jesus Christ shed for our redemption. By reading the words of Corinthians 11:23, and if you follow it through to the end of the chapter, you will gain an auditory experience, where we remember what took place on the night when Jesus was betrayed. However, it is through these specific foods that we connect the visual and auditory experience to provide better understanding of the immense sacrifice Jesus had to endure.

> *The grapes are crushed to produce the wine; so was Jesus crushed physically, emotionally, and in spirit to produce our salvation.*

The texture of the bread is dry, reminding us how Jesus Christ, while he hung on the cross, said, "I thirst". He died so that we do not have to thirst spiritually. We can always drink from the living water that Jesus Christ provided for us. And finally, we engage our sense of taste by tasting the bland wafer of bread and by tasting the juice from the grape. We recall that Jesus did it all for us; He did it all for you... He did it all for me. So, Jesus is God. Just as the father provided food as a way for us to remember what he did for the children of Israel, when he delivered them from the hands of Egyptian bondage and brought them into Canaan, the promised land. Jesus Christ included food in the feast day that remembers and honors him and by engaging all our five senses. He is helping us remember him the best way we can. The Father did it, Jesus did it, because Jesus is also God.

Take away: Take some time out to remember the important things in your life. It does not have to be a big expense of money. Whether it be a simple meal or a catered affair, the time you spend with loved ones over a meal will be priceless. The food and drinks will remind you of the event, and it will build precious memories with your loved ones. Take time to remember the Lord Jesus. Don't run from taking the Lord's supper. Confess your sins and shortcomings to him. Also, confess to the ones that you may have offended, and ask for forgiveness. It is time to enjoy all the benefits of partaking in the feast of Holy communion.

CHAPTER FIVE: MY FAVORITE BIBLE VERSE

I don't know if it's proper to have a favorite Bible verse because we live by every word that proceeds out of the mouth of God. However, at this current time in my life, there is a verse that speaks to me above all of the other verses in the Bible. It is Revelation 12:11, "And they overcame him by the blood of the Lamb, and by the word of their testimony; and they loved not their lives unto the death." This has become one of my favorite scriptures because it teaches us how to overcome the enemy. During my five-year period of isolation, the Lord revealed to me some truths through this scripture. Now, just before I give you the word that the Lord gave me, I want to share with you that I do listen to commentaries from Pastors, Teachers, and Rabbis because I love the word of God and I love to understand the meaning of what I'm reading. However, above all, I love it when the Lord personally gives me an interpretation of his word. There is nothing better to me in life than the

Lord taking a scripture and showing me the truth from it; a truth that is applicable to my daily life.

> *"And they overcame him by the blood of the Lamb, and by the word of their testimony; and they loved not their lives unto the death" (Rev. 12.11).*

Here is what I believe the Lord shared with me. He shared with me the power of our testimony. Shadrach, Michalak and Abednego loved not their lives unto death. When faced with the choice of worshiping the image that King Nebuchadnezzar had set up, and if not, they would have to face a certain death by fire, these three young men made the choice to defy the King and stand up for the Lord, God. The King questioned them and gave them a chance to speak, and they spoke to the King with respect; however, they told him that there is not a situation where they would bow to any idol. These three men let King Nebuchadnezzar know that they would only worship the God of heaven. In other words, they testified as to their belief in God, just as someone does in a courtroom. They bore witness to who God is, the power that he possesses, and their undying faith in him; knowing that even if he did not deliver them from the fire, they would not serve any other God. They kept the first and the most important commandment that God gave mankind. "Thou shalt have no other gods before me" (Exod. 20.3).

I believe that when God gives us a list, he gives it in order of importance. If we keep the first commandment, we will keep all the other Commandments.

The meaning behind the first commandment is that we should have no other God besides him. If we live by those words, we will not murder, bear false witness, etc. Our love and commitment to God, with the help and guidance of the Holy Spirit, will enable us to keep all of the other commandments. When we keep the law of the Lord, we exchange our way for his way, and we experience life as he designed it for us.

The testimony of Shadrach, Michalak and Abednego was so powerful that when they were thrown into the fire, God protected them and the men who threw them in the fire died due to the fervent heat of the furnace. They were thrown into the fire bound, yet they were seen by the King and others walking around in the midst of the fire, loosed. Then, the King decreed that he saw four people walking around, and the fourth person looked to be the Son of God. To me, this was a direct vision of Jesus. Oh, how our testimony can bring down the very presence of Jesus into our life! Therefore, when we face dire circumstances and we are presented with an opportunity to testify as to who is with us, and what he can do, and when we take a stand for him; he will come down and be with us, walk among us, set us free from our bonds. Even in the midst of our fiery situation, Jesus will have a relationship with us in which he speaks to us in the middle of the fire.

In the Old Testament, I see some references to the sons of God, which are heavenly creatures that were created by Him; however, the reference by King Nebuchadnezzar points to the Son of God as singular. This is a direct reference to Jesus Christ because in the Old Testament no one understood who Jesus Christ was, because he was not yet born. Who is the Messiah? Christ the Lord.

> *This is a direct reference to Jesus Christ because in the Old Testament no one understood who Jesus Christ was, because he was not yet born.*

The Lord also revealed to me that King Hezekiah, when faced with death, did not accept the decree that came from the Lord through prophet Isaiah. When the prophet Isaiah told the King that he must get his house in order because he was about to die, the Bible says that "the King turned his face to the wall and prayed to God" (Isa. 38.2). I see this prayer as a testimony. King Hezekiah reminded God that he (Hezekiah) was obedient; he did what God had asked him to do and at the end of his prayer he wept showing his sincerity. King Hezekiah overcame by the word of his testimony. Instead of testifying to people, he testified to God of his devotion and obedience.

No sooner did Isaiah leave the inner courtyard, the Lord told him to turn back around and tell King Hezekiah that he had added 15 more years to his life. King Hezekiah overcame by the word of his testimony. When we obey God, we can remind him of it. God likes to reward the faithful, God likes to reward the just, and God takes pleasure in those who take pleasure in the ways of the Lord.

The Lord showed me a unique perspective when it came to overcoming by the blood of the Lamb. As we may know, blood is extremely important to God. It is so important because God put life in the blood. This is one of the main reasons why he told the children of Israel not to drink blood. This is why if you lose a limb, you may not die, but if you lose a certain amount of blood, you will surely die. To God, blood speaks; blood has a clear voice. In the Bible we can read an example of how blood speaks to God. When Cain killed his brother, Abel, we see that God heard the voice of Abel's blood crying out to him from the field. (Gen. 4.8). In other words, the blood of Abel testified against Cain. God knew what Cain did, for the blood of Abel bore witness to it. To God, blood does not just contain life, it is an audible "tape recorder" or "black box" of what took place when life was taken.

When we say that we overcome by the blood of the lamb, we overcome because when Jesus shed his blood, and God heard the voice of his blood crying out from the ground. The blood of the Lamb testified to what Jesus had accomplished. God heard the voice of the blood of the Lamb because the blood of Jesus testified that the price of our redemption was paid in full. We overcome because the blood of Jesus testifies that the price was paid for our forgiveness. The blood of Jesus testifies that only his blood was sinless and was the only price that could be paid for our redemption. Just as the blood of Abel cried out from the field, the blood of Jesus cried out from the hill called Calvary.

Take away: If you want to overcome in your life, you must testify. You can testify by sharing with others what God has done for you or what God can do, based on your belief in his words. You can testify to God as to your obedience; not that we would be prideful or rely on our works. We can simply remind God that he is a rewarder of those who delight themselves in the law of the Lord. We also can overcome by reminding the enemy that Jesus' blood cries out to God, covering us and washing away every sin that we confess to him and every sin that we turn away from.

CHAPTER SIX: COMMITMENT

I realized that one of the biggest problems I had in life; one of the main things that had really set me back, was my lack of commitment. I became accustomed to not giving my best. I didn't give my best on the job; I didn't give my best in my previous marriage, and I didn't give the Lord God my best. What I did was, give people my best in spurts, instead of being consistent. Now, I understand it was that lack of commitment that hindered me from progressing in my life. There are several reasons why I was afraid to fully commit to things. The first reason is: I didn't want to be responsible if things didn't work out. It was so much easier for me to blame someone else when I did not take full responsibility for a decision that needed to be made. If it didn't work out, I could blame someone else for what I should have been responsible for. The second reason is: commitment takes consistent effort. The type of effort that enables you to see it through to the end. It's not easy to try and try and try again until you get your breakthrough. It was so much easier for me to give up in the middle, instead of seeing it through to the end. However, the result was always the same, failure and disappointment from the people that trusted me to see things through.

I was asked by the Pastor of a church in South River, New Jersey, to be their church musician and play for them on Sundays. I figured I needed to stay active in a church in order for me to have some type of connection to a church and the Lord, so I accepted the offer. Before long, not only was I the church musician where church service started around 11:00 AM, but I quickly became the Sunday school teacher, which basically means teaching Bible class on Sunday mornings starting at 10:00 AM. Most of the congregation came from the surrounding area. I had to travel from Maplewood, New Jersey, down to New Brunswick, New Jersey, and back then, faithful sisters from the church would pick me up and drive me over to the church for Sunday school. God was teaching me how to be committed. I seemed to be the furthest from the church, yet I would be one of the first to arrive there. Every Sunday, I voluntarily cleaned the bathroom. When it snowed, I shoveled the snow. When it was hot, I got there to turn on the air-conditioning. When it was cold, I remember many Sunday school classes starting out in the cold because it took the church a while to warm up after the heat kicked in. God was teaching me how to be committed.

> *God was teaching me how to be committed. I seemed to be the furthest from the church, yet I would be one of the first to arrive there.*

I had joined the church and after a while the Pastor gave me several opportunities to deliver the Sunday sermons. I was and I still am grateful for those opportunities. On those rare occasions when the pastor had to speak at another church on Sunday, he left me in charge. This is where I learned how to run a church service and function in the role of a Pastor, although I was never given any official title.

Because of my commitment to the church and to the Pastor, the Lord gave me the opportunity to serve in an office as a pastor; a role that I would later become ordained to function in. Opportunities to serve began to increase. The pastor allowed me to teach Bible class on Wednesdays. We saw many great signs and wonders. I remember one particular Wednesday evening, after we had Bible class, I was on my way home with a brother from the church. We were driving north on the Garden State Parkway. It was raining and dark. Suddenly, the brother who was sitting next to me, driving, took off his glasses and he put his glasses back on. Then he took them off again and started reading the license plates of the cars ahead of him. Now he was driving, so I was starting to get a little concerned…

I asked him, "Is everything OK?"

He answered, "My eyesight is better. I don't need my glasses to see distance anymore. I can actually read the license plates without my glasses and I couldn't do that before the service."

The Lord God blessed his vision, and he was able

to see better than he was able to see in years. During those years, the Lord would move in strange miraculous ways. It was so funny to see the congregation when the pastor started speaking. The pastor and I never discussed what the Sunday school teaching was going to be about, nor did we discuss what his Sunday sermon was going to be about. However, Sunday after Sunday, for months, when he got to a certain point in his sermon the congregation gave him that look as if they just heard what he was saying before he said it, and he would always look at the congregation and say with a smile on his face, "Oh, you heard that this morning..." The very scriptures that I would teach about earlier, he would preach about it later.

One night, we both experienced a demonic attack on the same night. If I remember correctly, it was a Thursday, and I was struggling to breathe in my sleep. It felt as if the enemy was choking me. I was about to suffocate and the only thing I could do was call out the name Jesus in my mind. As soon as I said Jesus as loud as I could in my mind, instantaneously, the enemy's hold was broken, and I was able to breathe normally again. When I shared that testimony with my pastor, he told me that he had experienced the same thing around the time I did. I believe that demonic attack came because the enemy saw that my level of commitment was increasing.

During my three years at that ministry, God enabled me to give words of knowledge and prophecy.

He enabled me to pray for the sick and see them healed. All of this, he did without me having any official title. I believe the main reason why this thing started to manifest in my life is because I changed my heart and started to become committed to God and the people in my life that I needed to be committed to.

As soon as I said Jesus as loud as I could in my mind, instantaneously, the enemy's hold was broken, and I was able to breathe normally again.

I remember the time God told me it was time to leave that church. I left the keyboard that I had purchased to play at the services, not realizing that it was symbolic because in the not-too-distant future, God would change my office from church musician to Pastor. It was a few years later, but I would see the confirmation of this.

My sister's birthday was soon approaching, and I asked her what she wanted for her birthday. The only thing she wanted was for me to visit one of the services at the church that she attended, to get a word from her pastor, who is a prophet. I agreed to attend. When the man of God touched me, he said that I was wearing the wrong shoes. He said that because I had been afraid to step into the full mantle of my ministry. Thus, the word he gave was correct. At that time, I was primarily known as a church musician. During the three years that I spent at that ministry in South River, New Jersey, God trained me to become a pastor. The Prophet said, "Your ministry has been delayed at least six years. You have a two-step office. When you are grounded as a pastor, God will move your office to the next step which is the Apostle." All these things start to fall in place because I decided to make a full commitment to the Lord, to the ministry, to whatever job God put in front of me, and I made a full commitment to all people that he surrounded me with.

Take away: If you want to overcome in your life, there's no getting around being committed. We must be committed to our relationship with our Lord Jesus Christ, we must be committed to our relationship with our spouse, our children, and we must be committed to the work that God has put before us. If we give a full commitment, the Lord will enable us to keep our word, and the people will see the glory of God through us. We become a pipeline through which God can bless people. As you may know, the pipe that delivers the water also gets wet on the inside. When God uses us to help others, we also are helped.

CHAPTER SEVEN: YOU WILL BE RESTORED

We often get discouraged when in life it seems that we have taken a major step back. If we have lost our job, it is devastating to us. If we go through a divorce, we often think about the mistakes that we had made and what we should've done differently. If we have suffered the death of a close loved one, it seems like the pain never completely goes away, and we wonder how to go on with such a giant hole in our lives. There are times in our life when we go through some type of devastating subtraction that causes us to wonder if we are still God's child and if he still has a plan for our lives.

In the Bible, King Nebuchadnezzar was the ruler of Babylon. At that time, he was the King of the World. Nebuchadnezzar struggled with a character flaw that many of us struggle with. We are challenged each day to overcome this destructive trait. King

Nebuchadnezzar struggled with too much pride. This form of pride caused him to be overly self-reliant and overly self-glorifying when he achieved some type of accomplishment. This pride caused him to forget that it was God that gave him all that he had. For this reason, he had a responsibility to consult God on decisions and give God the credit for his great victories.

In his day, King Nebuchadnezzar built one of the most impenetrable, yet beautiful cities the world has ever seen. To this day, people still talk about the Great Hanging Gardens of Babylon. In the book of Daniel, chapter 4, King Nebuchadnezzar gives his version of what happened to him. He was troubled about a dream that he had, and he brought all of his magicians, elders, and wisemen to help him understand the interpretation of the dream, yet, no one could interpret it for him. The last one to see the King was Daniel, a man that God had skilled with the ability to interpret dreams. Daniel was one of the captives from the tribe of Judah, taken in his youth to serve in the King's Court.

> *To this day, people still talk about the Great Hanging Gardens of Babylon.*

The King's dream showed a beautiful tree that grew tall and strong. Its branches reached up to heaven. It was so secure that the birds could find a place to rest, but there was a watcher and a holy one. The watcher decreed that the tree be cut down, but the stump was to remain, and it would remain for seven years. The stump would become a creature, like the beast of the field. This beast would be wet with the dew that watered the ground. His nails would grow into claws and he would become hairy and would no longer have the heart of a man, but the heart of a beast.

After hearing the interpretation of his dream, twelve months had passed. As King Nebuchadnezzar walked throughout looking at his beautiful kingdom, he asked himself, "Is not this great Babylon that I have built for the house of the kingdom, by the might of my power and for the honor of my majesty?" (Dan. 4.30). Daniel states in the Bible,

> While the word was in the King's mouth, he heard a voice from heaven saying, "Oh, King Nebuchadnezzar to thee it is spoken, the kingdom is departed from thee. And they shall drive thee from men, and thy dwelling shall be with the beasts of the field: they shall make thee to eat grass as oxen, and seven times shall pass over thee, until thou know that the most High ruleth in the kingdom of men and, giveth it to whomsoever he will. The same hour the thing was fulfilled upon Nebuchadnezzar (Dan. 4.31).

After seven times had passed over King Nebuchadnezzar, which is an old way of saying seven years, this man that ate grass like an animal; he grew hairy skin and nails that look like claws. This once glorious king was reduced to the form and nature of an animal. At the end of seven years, he communicated by lifting his head up to heaven and declared:

> I blessed the most High, and I praised and honored him that liveth for ever, whose dominion is an everlasting dominion, and his kingdom is from generation to generation; and all the inhabitants of the earth are reputed as nothing; and he doeth according to his will in the army of heaven, and among the inhabitants of the earth; and none can stay his hand, or say unto him, What doest thou? (Dan. 4.34-35).

When King Nebuchadnezzar made this declaration, the Lord God restored his kingdom to him. He did not have to fight for it. He didn't have to use political espionage to get it. It was just handed back to him when he gave God the praise and the glory and recognized that God gave him all that he had.

God will restore you when you understand that God has given you all that you have. Irrespective of your circumstance, He is worthy of all the glory, the honor, and the praise. I went from earning a six-figure salary as a sales manager for some of New York's largest radio stations, to packing boxes at Amazon for $16 an hour. I had a tremendous economic fall. I went from having a beautiful three-bedroom house in Maplewood, New Jersey to renting a room in Irvington, New Jersey. I went from having a family to living alone.

Irrespective of your circumstance, He is worthy of all the glory, the honor, and the praise.

There are times in our lives when we go through tremendous setbacks, but you do not have to let those difficult circumstances define you. The overcoming of those challenges should define you. During the setbacks, I continued to trust in the Lord. I still believed that God had a purpose for me and although on the outside, things looked bad, God was working on my inside. I was dropping my pride. I was allowing myself to become consistent and dedicated to doing the things that would help my family and strengthen my relationship with God. Now I can truly say that God is restoring me. Areas in my life that were lacking now have abundance. This turnaround, it's not due to my intelligence, or my connections, or an inheritance. I owe the turnaround completely to my Lord Jesus Christ and his patience with me during these formative years.

The years of suffering should be viewed as years of learning. The lessons that I have learned during my years of struggle can never be forgotten. Now, I have more confidence for the next set of trials. I know they will be difficult, but I know the Lord Jesus will be with me and as I overcome each trial. I will also gain some new insight that will enable me to be a better servant of Christ and help me to be of better service to my fellow men.

It's easy to think about giving up when things get very difficult; when we lose a family member; when we lose our job or when we have fallen into some type of pit that erodes all credibility. I want you to know that I am a living witness as to what can happen when you choose not to give up, when you choose to trust that the gifts that God has given you are for a purpose. When you choose to believe that the enemy can have power over you, you are actually choosing to disbelieve what God said. God said, "I will never leave you nor forsake you" (Deut. 31.6). God said, "I am a very present help in time of trouble" (Psalm. 46.1). He also said, "Trust in the Lord with all of your heart and lean not to your own understanding. In all thy ways acknowledge him and he will direct your path" (Prov. 3.5-6).

Take away: Just as the greatest character trait is Love, the worst character trait is Pride. Pride causes us to rely on ourselves, to rely on someone or something other than God. Pride breaks the most important commandment. We are to have no other God other than the most high God, Yahweh. Once we drop that spirit of pride, we will be able to walk the path to restoration and clearly see the good that comes out of learning from our missteps. No matter how bad it seems, remember that "...No good thing will he withhold from them that uprightly" (Psalm. 84.11).

CHAPTER EIGHT: THE CUP OF WATER

If I were to ask you to pick up a glass of water and put it to your lips and drink it, most of us would find it relatively easy. This is something we do in some form or fashion every day. For some of us it's coffee; for some of us it's tea; and for some it's soda. Hopefully, most of us drink water every day, it's essential for a healthy diet... but I digressed. Back to the topic. Picking up a glass of water and putting it to our lips for most of us it's no big deal. A young child can do it, although they may use two hands, but if you take that same cup of water and now you were asked to hold it for one hour without putting it down. Something that was so simple becomes difficult. If you were in a situation where your life depended on it and someone said that in order to save yourself or your loved one, you would have to hold a glass of water for one week without putting it down. As much as we would want to, I cannot imagine anyone that would pass that test. The weight of the glass and the water are the same as when we raise it up to our lips for a drink and put it down. Why is it more difficult? Obviously, the answer is time. Adding time to a simple situation can make the situation far worse to deal with. This is what happens when we allow certain weights in our life to get heavier due to the amount of time that passes; without resolving these weights.

> *Why is it more difficult? Obviously, the answer is time. Adding time to a simple situation can make the situation far worse to deal with.*

What is your weight? Is it unforgiveness? Is it jealousy? Is it insecurity? Or is it pride? The Bible says, "Lay aside every weight and the sin that doeth so easily beset us" (Heb. 12.1). Realizing that we have a weight and facing it or dealing with it quickly, will allow us to suffer minimal damage as opposed to us ignoring our shortcomings or feeding them. Whether we ignore it or feed it, we are allowing time to pass, and that length of time causes those weights to become heavier as they cause more destruction in our lives.

> *What is your weight? Is it unforgiveness? Is it jealousy? Is it insecurity? Or is it pride?*

Jealousy causes us to have a distorted view of reality. Pride puffs up, creating the lie that we are more important than the people that God has placed in our lives to serve. Insecurity causes us to sink into the abyss of despair, as if we were in quicksand. Unforgiveness puts up a barrier as big as the Chinese wall. Let me share with you how this thought pertains to me and how the Lord brought about a miracle that I thought I would never live to see.

As this book is being published and distributed, I'm in my mid-50s. From the time I was a child, I had a horrible issue of unforgiveness towards my father. There were things that he did that grieved me as they were things that I did that grieved him. When we moved to the United States from the United Kingdom, I was eight years old and placed in the second grade. It seems that the Lord God has gifted me in the area of speech and vocabulary. Through observing the world via TV, conversations, etc... I picked up on a lot of things that children my age did not pick up on. As a result, I was placed in a class for gifted youngsters in my middle school years. At that time, it was called the SP class and I was one of those students who wanted to skip a grade and so we were placed in a specialized program where we skipped the seventh grade so that we could be ready for high school. Although I did very well in subjects like English, I did poorly in subjects like Math.

When it came time for me to choose a high school, high school was chosen for me, which was a school where I could learn how to become an auto mechanic. I rejected that because I knew nothing about cars and had no interest in fixing them. However, there was a high school that I was very interested in, but it seemed to be an incredible longshot to get in. The high school was the LaGuardia High School of Music and Art in New York City, Manhattan. The school is currently located in Midtown Manhattan near the Lincoln Center for the Performing Arts. Back in my day, it was located in what looked like a castle on a hill around 135th St. in Harlem.

I met with my music teacher and told her that I wanted to try out for the High School of Music and Art. At the time, I was in her class learning to play the violin. I was such a newbie to the violin that I couldn't name the four strings correctly. I mentioned to her that I would like to try out for voice. Here I am, thirteen years of age with a sense of my calling. I am so glad that I pushed aside my fear and pushed towards the arena God called me to. My music teacher taught me "Bridge Over Troubled Water" by Paul Simon. I took the number 2 train from the Bronx to Manhattan, walked into the audition, and left the audition as the High School of Music and Art's newest student.

> *I am so glad that I pushed aside my fear and pushed towards the arena God called me to.*

Because of the conflicts I had with my father, I went out to defy him by doing the worst thing I possibly could do. I cut class, slacked up, and did not make the best of my opportunities. It was dumb, stupid, foolish, and every other adjective that could describe someone who made a bad choice. As a result, after my first year I got kicked out of the school because of my lack of attendance. I would show up on the days of tests and pass the tests with about a 70, but I was expelled because I did not complete the homework and did not show up for class. When my parents received the information, of course, they were disappointed and upset they had to enroll me in my local high school which was in the Bronx. The name of the high school was Evander Childs High School. This school was so different from what I was used to, as we called it, the High school of M & A. Instead of being treated as an adult, we were not allowed to leave the school grounds for lunch. I did not see the diversity in the student body or diversity throughout the teaching staff. It was a huge step down, but it was all my fault. This was one of many bad choices that I made up until my time of exile had ended.

October 2020, my father and I had a long discussion down in his home in Florida. It was very difficult for us to have a conversation because he is deaf. So, I would listen to him and try to type out on my laptop my answers and questions; quite tedious. One of the things that he brought up was one of the things that troubled him the most about me. He brought up my expulsion from the High School of Music and Art, how it hurt him, and that I left such a prestigious high school to be enrolled in a school that everyone in my area could get into. He shared some things with me that he never shared with me growing up all those years. He said the guidance counselor that he had to speak to, the person who enrolled me in my local high school, told him and my mother what a tremendous fall it was for me to leave such a prestigious high school and be enrolled in a local high school. As my father shared the story with me, he told me that I was brilliant as a child and how it hurt him that I squandered that opportunity.

As a poor boy growing up in Jamaica, he never had the opportunity to have a good education. One of his greatest wishes in life was to have an education and he never had the opportunity to get it. He often said that he wouldn't be able to read had it not been for the Bible. This is the first time in my life he ever told me that I was brilliant. I knew that I was gifted. The teachers knew that I was gifted. My fellow gifted students knew that I was gifted enough to belong. However, at the age of 55 that was the first time my father ever paid me a compliment like that.

> *One of his greatest wishes in life was to have an education and he never had the opportunity to get it. He often said that he wouldn't be able to read had it not been for the Bible.*

The next day, we had a terrible discussion because he was hard of hearing and I was sitting next to him with my laptop trying to express my thoughts in a way where he could read it from the laptop and, this was going nowhere... I mean nowhere. So, I went into the kitchen area to be with my wife, and my Dad, who is hard of hearing and suffering from chronic shoulder pain from a torn rotator cuff (that he does not want to get surgery for), comes out of the bedroom carrying something beige in his hands. He is walking out of the bedroom with this object like a ring bearer would carry the wedding rings on a black velvet pillow. His wife, my stepmom, rushed over to him and pushed him back into the room. She was saying, "Joe, this is nonsense." As she continues to push him back to the bedroom. I only got a glimpse of the object and asked her what it was. She said it was a stone. It happened so quickly that my mind imagined a beige stone, but Elina was able to see what it was from her angle. It was a handgun covered in beige cloth. Dad went back into the room and came back out without the object. Now, I understand that Dad was so distraught, he was in so much physical and emotional pain that he wanted me to kill him. Thus, putting him out of his misery. Drama! A few moments later, Elina went into the guest bedroom where we were staying. I went into the bedroom where my wife was sitting and reading Psalm 51.

I turned on Psalm 51 and played it through biblegateway.com on my laptop, so we both could hear it. I started praying to the Lord saying, "Lord, I've done all I could do. I have humbled myself seeking for him to admit his ways; seeking for him to apologize".

During previous conversations earlier that day, I apologized to him for all the wrong that I have done to him and for all of the things that I did that disappointed him. I wrote it down so he could hold it. Still, no apology from him. So, here I am praying in the room with my wife, saying, "Lord, what more can I do?"

I felt like packing up the bags and getting an early flight back to New Jersey. When suddenly, my father walked into the room, sat on the bed, and wanted to have a conversation. In my heart I was like, "Oh, my God... here we go again." The last two conversations ended up in raised voices, frowned up faces, and me walking away to avoid further conflict. However, this time it was different.

I was always curious to know what happened to him when he left Jamaica at 14 years of age and ended up in England, marrying my mother, and having me in 1965 when he was around 23 years old... Well, this was the day I got the chance to hear it. As he sat on the bed, he began to tell the story. He shared how he left to make his way in life. At 14 years of age, he was able to pay to get on a boat and take that long trip from Jamaica to the United Kingdom. His father sold a parcel of land to give him the money. He shared things that happened along the way, which I was dying to know about. After he shared the story, he said how proud he is of me, my sister and my other three brothers. Tears began to run down his face, tears began to run down my face, and he put his hand on my head and told me that he forgives me and that he loves me. I gave him a kiss on the neck and a hug. The wall was broken, and the floodgates came crashing down. Nothing but tears, hugs, and love. We had both been carrying that cup of water too long. It seems that we were never going to get to the place where we could put that cup down, but praise be to God. The Lord knows how to answer prayers.

Many times, when we pray, the answer does not come instantly. Please, don't misunderstand me. I know the Lord can do miracles. I've witnessed many of them myself. Times when he has instantaneously healed and delivered, and I will share some of these miracles later, in upcoming chapters. However, there are some things in our life that take time. We must go through the process, to develop our perseverance, peace, and faith in God. I am pleased to say that we no longer hold that cup of bitterness, which we have both held for over 47 years. My arms were tired from holding that cup, my heart was becoming calloused from holding it and my perspective was skewed by holding that cup. But now that I have let it go, I am free. I never received an apology from my father, and I never will. In his dictionary, the word apology does not exist! And guess what? At this point, I could care less. It doesn't matter. I know that I have forgiven him, and the weight is released from my life and I believe that now, I can move forward in the full power and mantle of what the Lord has waiting for me as I daily step into my destiny.

Take away: Don't let time make your situation worse. Procrastination is a dangerous weight. As difficult as it may be, face your issue. If you are willing, He is able to get you through it. God said, "When thou passest through the waters, I will be with thee; and through the rivers, they shall not overflow thee: when thou walkest through the fire, thou shalt not be burned; neither shall the flame kindle upon thee" (Isa. 43:2).

CHAPTER NINE: THE 2020 CHRISTMAS MIRACLE, ONE OF MANY

I believe in the power of tithing. I know that there are many people out there that believe that this is an Old Testament teaching. Many believe that tithing does not apply to us. For those who live under the New Testament, Jesus said in the book of Matthew:

> Woe unto you, scribes and Pharisees, hypocrites! For ye pay tithe of mint and anise and cumin, and have omitted the weightier matters of the law, judgment, mercy, and faith: these ought ye to have done, and not to leave

the other undone. (Matt. 23.23)

Jesus scolded the Pharisees, for they gave tithe of their material wealth, but did not give God that which was even more important than the tithe. God wanted the Pharisees to treat people fairly in regard to the Law and judgment. God wanted the religious Jewish leadership to exercise mercy and faith towards others, and not leave out the tithe. With Jesus, it was not an either-or proposition. He wants us to do both; give back to God from our material increase, that which is his, the tithe or 10% of our income. But also, judge wisely, treat poor people with mercy and use faith in the word of God to make good decisions. Ever since my wife Elina and I got married, we have committed to tithing.

I can't speak for anyone else, but I can testify to the fact that ever since we started tithing, the Lord has always provided for us. We may not receive everything that we want or when we want it, but we certainly have received more than enough to meet our needs.

Spirit and Truth Center for Worship, Inc. was founded in November 2019. By November 2019, we had five members including my wife and myself. Each week we had a few visitors, but the Lord God blessed each Sunday service, and he blessed us each Wednesday night amid Bible study. During December 2020, Elina and I were both receiving unemployment. We both lost out on our job opportunities due to the Coronavirus pandemic of 2019-2020. We had paid all of our bills for the month of December, but we weren't sure how we were going to eat. We never told anyone that we were going through this test and we continued to praise God as we gave to the Lord the 10% that was due to him.

We both lost out on our job opportunities due to the Coronavirus pandemic of 2019-2020.

It was on December 23rd when we received a phone call from our Deacon. He said he needed to pass by and drop something off to us. So we said, "Come on over."

Not having a clue as to what was about to happen. He pulled up to the house and put a card in my hand. Since it was from the congregation, I walked upstairs and handed the card to Elina so that she could open it. Tears began to stream down her face. She thanked the Lord and handed me the card. It was a beautiful card signed by the members and friends of the ministry with a cash donation of $250. Two hundred and fifty dollars may not sound like much to many of the people that are reading this book, but for two people who didn't know how they were going to eat, it meant the world. We were able to give the Lord his tithe and head out to the grocery store and put some food in the refrigerator and freezer. To this day, we never told the congregation that we're in such dire need. The only way they will know is by reading this book, just like you.

Elina has experienced many miracles like this. I remember that very early in our relationship, I needed a car. We have both worked for Amazon packing boxes. We both made around $16 an hour. I would have to take a bus from Irvington, New Jersey to Newark, Penn Station, New Jersey. Once there, we would have to wait for a shuttle bus from Newark, New Jersey to Edison, New Jersey where we would be dropped off at the Edison warehouse. This whole process would take about two hours. If I had a car, the drive door to door (depending on traffic) would be about 40 minutes. I was losing out on valuable sleep not to mention the aggravation of public transportation; having to deal with people that had loud cell phone conversations without using headphones, while having to deal with buses that always ran late whenever it rained or snowed. One day, Elina said to me, "We really need a car." She asked me what kind of car I wanted. Anyone that knows me knows that I believe God and I have a whole lot of faith. The problem was, I didn't have any money. But she asked me, so I gave her an answer. I wanted a used Porsche Cayenne. If you're familiar with that car, you would understand that it was way out of my budget. Not to mention that I would have no way to pay for parts and labor if it needed repairs. She thought I was out of my mind.

That night she went to work, and the Lord went to work. One of her coworkers was a car enthusiast, and a bit of a know it all… If you know what I mean. She mentioned to him the type of car that I wanted, and it's as if the Lord put a fire in him to find the right car for us. Instead of spending all his time doing his job, he spent most of that night on the Internet looking for the right type of car. He told Elina of the type of car that he thought would be perfect for us and it was not a Porsche Cayenne, but he had a car that had similar specs and cost a whole lot less and it would be much easier to repair. He recommended an Audi Q5.

> *She mentioned to him the type of car that I wanted, and it's as if the Lord put a fire in him to find the right car for us.*

When it was time for Elina to have her lunch break, she called me and told me what her friend recommended. She thought that I would be very disappointed because it was not a Porsche Cayenne. I was not familiar with the vehicle so she sent over a picture, and when I saw it, I knew that it would be the right car for us. To Elina's surprise, I told her that this would be great. She told her friend and he continued to search for the best prices in the area. He eventually found a car that was in an Audi dealership which was located in Edison, New Jersey, very close to the warehouse from where we worked.

Shortly after, we were searching for that car on the Internet, trusting that the Lord would give it to us. The car was listed for over $11,000 and when we checked our credit and the amount of money we had, we found out that all we had was $1,000 that we could put down on the car. Monthly car payments would be out of my budget. In order for the payments to be affordable for me, I would need to purchase the car for no more than $8,000. When I told Elina that I believe God would give us this car for $8,000, she said that was impossible. This is where my world-famous line came from: "I don't know how, I don't know when, but I know he will". I have worked in sales all my life and I knew enough to wait until the end of the month to go to the dealership to try to negotiate a deal. So, that is what I did, knowing that some salesperson needed the sale to make their monthly goal and that they would be more likely to work with me to accomplish their goals.

We pulled into the parking lot and the plan was to put $1,000 down on the credit card and finance the rest. As we sat in the parking lot, Elina wanted to transfer some money from one account to an account that helped to pay for her father's living expenses out there in Puerto Rico. I did not disagree, but in my mind, I didn't think that this was great timing. Here we were, getting ready to do battle with some car dealer and she's working on something else, but I didn't know what the Lord was about to do next. As she went to her account to transfer some money to the other account, she noticed a $5,000 increase. She had filed her taxes after several people that she knew. Yet, she received the money in her account as we were sitting in the parking lot. She was in shock, but I knew the Lord was at work. This way we did not have to put $1,000 down on a credit card.

We could just put that money down in cash.

We walked into the car dealership and I went over to a salesperson who had a brown skin color like me, figuring that many people would pass him by and not give him an opportunity. We sat down and showed him the vehicle that we were interested in from the internet. He went out to the parking lot and pulled up in a black Audi Q5. The color of the seats were the same color as we had seen in the picture; they were a beautiful tan color. We went back inside and started to negotiate.

He started off with a price of $13,000. I told him, "That was not the price that we had listed here from the Internet." The price that we had seen in the picture was $11,000. I took a good look at the car and I could see scratches on the outside of the passenger door. The scratches were unusual because they were curly cue scratches like a pig's tail, and then the car spoke to me. The car said, "Girl... You can't trust him! He's a liar." As if some angry woman keyed the car as an act of revenge. I told the car dealer that it was not the correct price and he replied that perhaps he had the wrong car.

> *The car said, "Girl... You can't trust him! He's a liar." As if some angry woman keyed the car as an act of revenge.*

He went back to the parking lot and pulled up with another Black Audi Q5. This car had gray seats instead of the tan seats, which we had seen in the picture. The car needed four new tires, it was missing a seat belt in the back, and it looked like it needed a paint job. The finish of the car was very dusty looking, but this was the car they were offering for $11,000.

I explained to the car dealer all of the problems that I could see with the car. The tires, the seat belt in the back and the dusty looking exterior paint job. I told him that I was also in sales, and that I could not pull up to one of my clients in a car that looked like that. The first thing that I would be thinking about once I purchased the vehicle was how much I would have to invest to fix it up. I told him I needed the car for no more than $8,000. He told me that they carefully compared the prices of their vehicles to all the prices on the Internet in the surrounding area and that we were going to find this vehicle for a lower price. I mentioned to the car dealer that we were there to buy a car and it was a Friday, that we were going to be in a car by Sunday, and the only question was if we were going to buy a car from him. Again, he told me that this was the best price. I looked at Elina and said, "Okay, honey. Let's go." and I got up to leave.

The salesman immediately asked us to hold on and wait a minute and allow him to speak with his manager. He went to the back and brought up the tall, handsome, dark-skinned manager. There was another man and woman, a couple, a few feet away from us trying to negotiate a car and they brought out the tall handsome Caucasian manager for them. Hm? I sat down and told the sales manager the same thing that I told the salesman. I mentioned the condition of the vehicle in great detail. I explained that I could not pull up to a client in a car which looked like that. I told the sales manager that I would like to buy this car and asked him if he wanted to sell me this car. He answered in the affirmative. I continued to ask him to help me, so that I could help him. The manager requested to let him go back to his office and see if he could work something out.

Fifteen minutes after, the salesman walked up to us and said, "Whose hands do I shake; you've got the car." He took us to the person who works out the paperwork. It was a 2011 Audi Q5 that had about 125,000 miles on it. The total bill for the car came up to a few dollars shy of $8,000. Just as we had prayed for. We had to wait a few hours for them to get the car ready for us. When we returned to the dealership, they had cleaned up the car. I don't know what they did to the outer body of the car, but it looked so much better than when it was sitting in the parking lot. They placed the key in my hands, and we drove off the lot, up Route One North. That was a mentally draining experience, but we were praising God as we drove up the road.

I asked Elina if she was hungry and we both agreed to try to find an Applebee's restaurant to celebrate what God had done. After driving for a few minutes without finding it, I noticed a restaurant called Little

Italy. Once we pulled in, I asked Elina if it would be ok to eat there. I drove off Route One and drove into the parking lot. We got out of the car and walked up to the door, when a man greeted us and apologized because it was a brand-new restaurant and it was getting ready to be opened. Soon after, he said that if we came inside, they would give us free food and drinks. They just wanted us to let them know if we liked the food and if we didn't, what changes we would recommend. In my mind I said, "What? Free food?" Of course, we agreed, and walked inside. The interior was beautiful. They proceeded to feed us an amazing salad followed by Brick Oven Pizza, Chicken Marsala and water imported from Naples, Italy. I felt so guilty for eating such an amazing meal that I left a generous tip for the waitress. They gave us enough food where we both had a doggie bag to take home with us. This is what the Lord did for us.

> *Suddenly after, he said that if we came inside, they would give us free food and drinks.*

Jesus deserves all the praise, all the credit for what took place that day. I believe what God's word says. I know without a doubt that if I bring the tithe and offering to the house of God, that he will rebuke the devour for my sake.

Take away: I believe that the act of tithing brings blessings into your life. When you return to God 10% of your gross income, your tithe becomes the representative or ambassador of your income, and

God blesses the 90% you have left. God finds ways to save your money and/or He finds ways to add increase to you. I am a living witness to the power of God's math. It's not logical for it works supernaturally. I know it's hard to start. This requires faith. I challenge you to try it for one month. You can test God in this area. God will come through for you because he does not go back on his word.

CHAPTER TEN: A GREAT WAY TO OVERCOME SIN AND ADDICTIONS

I was born on June 9th, 1965... it was a Wednesday. Born in Aldershot, a town located in Hampshire, England; it is about 31 miles southwest of London. I have fond memories of the eight years that I spent in England. Watching kids shows on TV like Dr. Who, H.R. Pufnstuf, and Vision On. I remember picking and eating gooseberries from my cousin's backyard, fish and chips, going to the seashore (you probably call it the beach) and amazing days in school. All of that came to an abrupt change when in March of 1973, my father and mother, sister, two brothers, and my youngest brother who my mother was pregnant with at the time, boarded a BOAC jet plane and moved to New York. We stayed in Mount Vernon, New York, for a couple of months with family until my parents were able to secure employment and a place for us to stay. When we were able to move, we moved to an apartment building in the South Bronx. It was quite a transition, moving from a house with a front yard and backyard to an apartment building that didn't have nearly the same amount of space. As a child, you don't ask questions, you just learn to go with the flow.

My father was always active in the church, even back in England. So, it wasn't strange that one of the first things that he sought out was a church where we could worship. This wasn't a big church where you could get lost in, you know, one of those churches where you can just sit in the back and nobody really knows you're there. This one was different. People passed by and they would smile; some even waved or shook your hand. It was the type of church where you couldn't remain anonymous. He had to pick the small storefront church where there were very few people, where you would have to participate. The pastor was a woman, Reverend Barkley and her husband was Deacon Barkley. I must've been around nine years old when I heard her preach a message and found my feet walking down towards the altar to accept Jesus Christ as my savior. I did this same thing the following Sunday just to be sure.

> *He had to pick the small storefront church where there were very few people, where you would have to participate.*

At the age of nine, I felt God's calling and I responded. During my entire life, the churches that I've been associated with, were churches that believed in the infilling of the Holy Spirit: speaking in tongues, healing, prophecy, etc... These churches always had a very strong message telling congregants not to sin. As a teenager, I was puzzled by all of these messages telling us not to sin and telling us about the consequence of sin, yet when I looked around, I would see my teenage companions pregnant; I would hear the jealousy and pride in the adults. I kept saying to myself, "Something is not adding up here. If we are being taught not to sin and the consequence of sin, why are we having all of these problems in our churches?" It wasn't until later in life that the Lord answered this question. To me, these are some of the greatest words ever spoken by the Lord, Jesus Christ. The book of Matthew says,

> Jesus said unto him, Thou shalt love the Lord thy God with all thy heart, and with all thy soul, and with all thy mind. This is the first and great commandment. And the second is like unto it, Thou shalt love thy neighbor as thyself
> (Matt. 22.37-39).

In that moment, I understood how the Lord Jesus wants us to overcome sin and temptation. He wants us to develop a love for him, a love for our fellow man and a love for ourselves. If we love God, we would not want to disappoint him, we would not want to remove ourselves from his favor; if we love God, we would not want sin to block us from his presence. If we love our fellow men, we would want to serve them, we would have compassion for them, and we would not want to sin against them and cause them harm. If we love ourselves, we would not want sin to harm us physically, financially, emotionally or in any other way.

The motivation that I was under was fear. The teachers and preachers used to teach the fear of hell to motivate one to live a righteous life, but it didn't work because some sin degrades you slowly and some sin erodes your relationship. Over a long period of time, it ruins you financially, dollar by dollar, instead of hundreds of dollars at the time. The longer the consequences take, the more risks people take, thinking that judgment is not going to come. That's why people don't expect it when judgment appears.

The right motivation is to love God, to love your neighbor and to love yourself. Yes, we are to have a holy fear of God, which can be interpreted as reverence or respect. However, I have found it much better to do things for the Lord based on love than to try to avoid his wrath by making decisions out of fear. My love for him develops into intimacy when I spend quality time with him. When I share with him my thoughts and feelings, and when I wait for him to share his with me, whether it be through a still small voice in my head, a dream at night, a vision in the daytime, or even the revelation that comes through reading his holy words, I still wait patiently for his answer. My love for him grows and that's the best motivator. I strive to live a life that is pleasing to him and rewarding to me. The moments of intimacy with the Lord are so special, you will remember them for the rest of your life.

I remember one day, my wife, Elina and I went to our nearest mountain to pray. It was South Mountain in South Orange, New Jersey. After praying, we noticed the smell of Myrrh in the air. The fragrance was familiar to me because I use Myrrh mixed with olive oil as an anointing oil when I pray for the sick. We started walking around like bloodhounds sniffing every tree bark and every flower around to see where the fragrance was coming from, but couldn't find it. We have no idea where it came from and where it went, but we both felt like we were on top of the mountain enjoying the presence of God; enjoying the aroma of God. As we worshiped him and thanked him, another fragrance made its way to us. This time, it was a sweet smell. I asked Elina if she could smell a funnel cake aroma. She answered that it smelled sweet, but she didn't know what a funnel cake smelled like. I smiled as we continued to spend time in the Lord's presence and thinking that he loved us enough to manifest himself in such an unusual way, a way that we would never forget.

I remember one day, my wife, Elina and I went to our nearest mountain to pray.

The next day I took Elina down to the Jersey shore so that she could experience her first funnel cake. We also had some of the world's best pizza. Yes, I'm biased. When you live in the New York area, you're going to experience great pizza, but I believe some of the best Pizza is Jersey Shore Pizza.

These types of experiences are not derived from fear. They come from developing a love for the Lord and our fellow man and ourselves. To develop our love for the Lord, we have to be like David. You have to spend time wooing the Lord. He loves to hear us testify about the great things he's done for us. He loves to hear us sing his praises. He loves when we clap our hands, dance, and shout before him. The more we spend this type of quality time with the Lord, the more he will find amazing ways to manifest his presence in our lives.

Take away: I have discovered that the key principle to success is motivation. No matter how knowledgeable, skilled, or politically connected one may be, if they are not motivated to succeed, they will not succeed. Let your love for Jesus be your motivation. Don't focus on a god that is looking to judge you, find you guilty and punish you for your mistakes. Focus on the Savior who loves you and is looking to reward your obedience. John, a beloved Apostle of the Lord, states in the Bible the following,"For God sent not his Son into the world to condemn the world; but that the world through him might be saved" (Jhn. 3.17).

CHAPTER ELEVEN: A GIFT

I believe that God has gifted everyone with the ability to do something that will help mankind and give God glory at the same time. Many people call this a gift. Some call this an anointing. I define this gifting or anointing as God's supernatural wisdom, knowledge and understanding in a particular area. Whether it is in the area of the science or the arts, whether it be philosophy or strategy. God has given everyone a particular skill, understanding that their strength is in an area of their lives that others see, and from where others can benefit.

I believe the Lord God has given me a gift in the area of communication. I seem to thrive when I'm doing something in the area of communication. I could be speaking in front of the congregation or having a one-on-one conversation. I could be singing or playing music if it has to do with communicating. It's usually an area where I feel very comfortable. I did not always feel comfortable with the gifts that the Lord God had given me. From very early in my life, I always had the ability to retain information quickly. I could watch a TV show where someone would speak and I would retain that information, process it quickly and come to an understanding. As I grew older, I realized that my gift had a lot to do with my ability to hear.

I often ask people which is the sense that they could not live without, if they had to lose one of their senses. Most people say to me that it's their ability to see. They need to be able to see what is going on in the world to be able to function in it. What a surprise when I tell them that for me, the sense I could not do without is my ability to hear. I figure I could get around if I couldn't see, but I would not be able to communicate without the ability to hear. Another question that I'm often asked is, "How do I know what my gift is?" I believe your gift is attracted to a problem that you were designed to solve. Let me share with you one of my experiences and then I'll give you a biblical example.

"How do I know what my gift is?"

When I was about 12 years old, a gentleman in the little Pentecostal church that we attended in the Bronx decided to put together a singing group. It was a way to keep the youth engaged and develop some of our talents and bring some notoriety to the church that we attended. At first, we were called The Little Group. After I had moved and my father, who was a deacon, was promoted to evangelist and transferred to a church in Yonkers, New York, the group became known as The Overcomers. Nonetheless, getting back to the calling and how your gifts show up in the time of problems. This group had two musicians: one was a guitarist, and the other was the drummer. They rehearsed with us and they were expected to play when we visited other churches. It was one evening and we were getting ready to sing, but we noticed the guitarist didn't show up. Everybody was wondering where he was. This happened in the 1970's; before cell phones were in use. So, there was no way to send a text or make a phone call. We were left in the dark wondering if he was going to show up.

As the minutes ticked by, it was time for us to get up and sing, and of course we were nervous. Being in a new place made us highly strung and to make matters worse, now we were going to sing without any music... So, we got up and started singing. As I was singing the first verse, I felt this burning in my chest that sent me over to the piano and played it. I had never played out in public before. I took a few piano lessons, but failed miserably because the teacher would put music in front of me and I would start playing it, and then she would take the music off the stand, and I would continue playing it.

I had never played out in public before.

I remember very clearly, the evening my father came to pick me up and the music teacher told him that she wasn't giving me any more music lessons because I was not reading the music. I was playing by ear. When the teacher played the music, I didn't realize what I was doing, but I had the ability to hear what she was doing and mimic it based on my memory. I would sit at home and listen to songs on the radio and noodle around on the piano and kind of pick out the chords and melody of what I was hearing. This was a secret to everyone else. So, as I stood up singing with the group, I kept feeling this pushing in my heart and the thought of going over to the piano. I was wrestling with the Lord because I never did this before, but the problem brought out the gift.

I nervously walked over to the upright piano and as I'm walking over, I heard everyone in my head saying, "What is he doing?" because I'm saying in my head "What am I doing?" I figured out that the song was in the key of F and for some reason I understood when the song was changing, and that I needed to B flat major or when I needed to go to C major and when I needed to go back to F major. If you would ask me how I knew at that time, at 12 years of age, I could not tell you. I just knew what to do. I just knew what fit. It was the problem that called out to me; it was the problem that allowed my gifts to manifest.

Something similar happened to King David when he was a young man. David had many gifts, but I believe the gift that propelled David to the throne was his ability to fight. David probably did not know that he had this ability. But when a problem arose, David's gifts arose to meet the challenge.

Before David became king, he was a shepherd boy. Probably looked down upon by his older brothers because he wasn't the biggest and he had a healthy curiosity. During that time in history, taking care of sheep was considered a lowly profession. There was not much dignity, not much respect came from tending sheep. But David made the best of a less than glamorous situation. David would spend his time in the wilderness as he took care of the sheep praising God; he would spend time praising God on the mountain, praising God in the meadow, while lifting his hands, dancing, and playing the harp to God. He aggressively sought the Lord so earnestly, that the Lord said, "I have found the man who is after my own heart" (Acts. 13.22). It was God's love for David that gave David his name, for the name David means beloved. David was beloved by God. Because of this intense relationship that David had with God, God gave him a gift that would propel him to the throne.

One day, while taking care of the sheep, he faced a bear. David hit the bear, defeated the bear, and protected the sheep. On another occasion, he faced a lion, and the Bible says that David chased down the lion, pulled him by his beard, rescued the sheep, struck the lion, and defeated him. However, notice when David's gift presented itself. It happened at the moment of David's Great Conflict... I'm sure that, like me, he was nervous to exercise his gift. David wasn't sure what the outcome would be, but, like me, I believe there was a pushing but tugging in his spirit to get what was rightfully his. His father Jesse had interested him with the sheep and David took that responsibility seriously. David could be trusted in the small matter of sheep... and so the Lord God developed those same skills, skills which made him ruler of Israel and Judah. The two battles that David had with the wild beasts were confidence boosters! It was preparation for one of his greatest battles that he would stand out in the valley of Elam and beat his greatest enemy, the mighty Goliath.

What has the Lord prepared you for? What problems have come your way that you have been given a God given ability to solve? What seems to be the recurring problem that you must overcome time and time again? When you discover that, you will discover your gifts and your skill set. The supernatural wisdom, knowledge and understanding in an area specifically targeted to help you overcome that recurring problem that faces you.

I have learned that I am not to use my gifts and talents to make money. Deriving an income from my gifts and talents only works when I use my gifts and talents to serve others and give God the glory at the same time. My motivation is always "how can I serve or how can I help?" We often run into trouble when we discover that we are gifted or talented in a certain area and go after the money instead of going after service. That approach always backfires because people are always looking for solutions. That's why the Lord God created you. The Lord God wants you to be a solution to a particular problem that you are gifted to solve. Find the problem and be the solution!

Another problem that we often run into when we discover what our gifts and talents is our desire to copy someone that has been successful. If we have a gift to heal, we try to do things like Oral Roberts or Kathryn Kuhlman. Thinking if we do it exactly like the person who came before us, we'll have the same results. It does not work that way. The Lord God trained Joshua to lead the children of Israel into the promised land. God said that he would be with Joshua as he was with Moses. But Joshua never received 10 Commandments, Joshua never parted the Red Sea, Joshua never lifted a brazen serpent in the wilderness so that the children of Israel who looked upon it would get healed. The gift of leadership was passed onto Joshua. Nevertheless, God used Joshua's personality, perspective, and voice to face his unique set of problems and work out unique victories. That's why, through Joshua, the children of Israel were able to pass through the Jordan River, break down the walls of Jericho, experience time standing still until they won the battle and then entered the promised land of Canaan.

> *Another problem that we often run into when we discover what our gifts and talents are, is our desire to copy someone that has been successful.*

Your gifts must be developed, and they can only

be developed through combat. That's why certain trials come your way; that's why you go through certain tests that help you depend on the Lord as you sharpen your talents and gifts. If you don't use your gifts, God will not take them away. God said that his gifts are given without repentance. (Rom. 11.29). Meaning, God will not repent or turn back from giving you your gifts; however, if you do not exercise your gifts, it is as someone that has a knife and does not sharpen it… it loses the ability to cut. You must exercise your gift. The Bible says, "...Work out your salvation with fear and trembling" (Phil. 2.12). Work out your calling with reverence for the Lord and respect for the power that you have and for how your gifts and talents can positively or negatively affect people.

My closing point on the subject is to recognize the one thing that can stop you is the spirit of fear. There are so many things that could be accomplished for the Lord if we would only listen to the Holy Spirit and not the spirit of fear. For we know that God has not given us the spirit of fear, but the power of love and a sound mind. Fear makes us forget that the Lord loves us and clouds our mind with self-doubt and doubt in God's ability to see us through. Be like Joshua. Be strong and courageous and know that the Lord is with you. He would not have given you these gifts and talents if he did not already foresee how you would be an asset to mankind and an asset to the Kingdom of God. Dedicate those gifts and talents to him and to serving others.

Take away: Recognize the recurring problems in your life. What are the same problems that different people present you with? What is the area where people pay you to do something that they find hard to do, but seems natural to you? Answer these questions and you will uncover your gift. You will find the place where you were designed to provide solutions that benefit mankind and glorify God at the same time.

CHAPTER TWELVE: GIVE SACRIFICIALLY (LOVE)

A few years ago, I got a call from my former wife. It was while I was still working for Home Depot in the flooring department. I remember it was during lunch time, so I went outside to take the call and she was crying.

This was a few years after our separation and things between us were not in a good place. She was on dialysis. This process removes the blood, purifies it, and sends it back into her because her kidney was failing. She had this procedure twice a week, and I never understood until then that people who are on dialysis go through a struggle each time. She explained how it felt like the machine was sucking the life out of her. She shared how many people have died on the dialysis machine and had suffered incredible depression while going through the procedure. But the reason why she called me crying was because both me and one of my brothers, my brother who lives out in Michigan, decided that we would be willing to donate a kidney if we passed the physical test. My brother is about three years younger than me and in better physical shape. He used to play college football for the University of Michigan, but for some strange reason, he wasn't able to go through the procedure because there was a small amount of hypertension detected. And so, she called me up crying because I was the only one left to donate a kidney and she wasn't sure that I would do it because of the status of our relationship.

Now I have to say, I share this not to give myself any praise, but just to point out what God can do when you decide to give sacrificially, even when going through a divorce. After hearing her concern, without hesitation, I reassured her that I would be willing to go through with the procedure. I let her know that I had made a commitment to this and I intended to carry it out.

> *She shared how many people have died on the dialysis machine and had suffered incredible depression while going through the procedure.*

God had always blessed me with good health. I'm in my mid 50's now and I never had an overnight stay at the hospital until I had the kidney surgery. So, the thought of an overnight stay in the hospital was a very new thought for me. After taking all of the tests and passing, I had to go to some psychological analysis. It felt to me as if the counselor was consistently trying to talk me out of doing this. She would give me all the reasons why I shouldn't do it. However, I kept on insisting that this is a choice I've made, and I wanted to do it.

At the time, my former wife didn't even understand why I was doing it. It didn't make any sense from an emotional standpoint, especially knowing how far apart we were. But when you love someone, it transcends superficial feelings; it transcends hurt of the past and it transcends current disappointments. I was able to look back at 30 years of marriage and appreciate all the sacrifices that she made for my children. If she passed away, there would not be another person that would give them the support that she would. I also looked at the sacrifices that she had made for me and I came to the decision that she was worth saving. Even if I had to die in the attempt. In my opinion, the things that she did for my children, for me, and for our Maplewood, N.J. community, earned her a second chance. So, without hesitation when she called me crying on that day, I let her know that I was willing to go through with the procedure. This decision did not come without a personal cost. This was during the time in my life when everything seemed to be falling apart.

> *It felt to me as if the counselor was consistently trying to talk me out of doing this.*

After giving the child support payments that

she and I agreed upon and paying for rent, I was left with very little money to buy food and to take the bus to work. I was recovering from surgery. I remember many days getting up at 4:15 AM and leaving by 4:30 AM to walk to work. I had to walk because I had so little money left. It was either walk or take the bus and if I took the bus, I wouldn't be able to eat. Being 6 feet tall, my weight dropped down to about 176 pounds. My walk to work took about an hour and a half through cold and snow to rain. I was determined to make my child support payment no matter what. So, every morning I would brave the 5.4-mile journey to work. After the kidney surgery, there were days where I would punch my timeclock and go to the bathroom, only to see blood mixed in my urine. I would have to walk up and down the concrete floors of Home Depot all day serving customers, lifting heavy boxes of tiles, only to walk the 5.4 miles back. Those were difficult days. Often, I would say to the Lord, "I'm giving my all." I was grateful that he loved me, but I had wondered if I was disqualified from being all the things that I believed that I could be for the Lord. Now, I know that years later, God honored those sacrifices. After I had left Home Depot and started working for Amazon packing boxes, God would show me how he honored the sacrifices of the past.

I met Elina, my wife, November 25th, 2018 and from that day forward, my life has changed for the better. We have the experience of God's miracle working power over and over again. He has delivered us out of financial distress. He has allowed us to smell a fragrance sent by the Lord, a fragrance that smells like myrrh. He has given us a congregation to shepherd without having the money to rent the building. He has provided us a way to give food and clothing out to others for free. He has done so many wondrous things for us and I can't help but believe that some of it was God's way of honoring the sacrifices that Elina and I have both made in the past.

If you are someone who is going through or has gone through a divorce, your life has not ended. There are many more chapters added to the book of your life. You can come through a divorce with a greater determination to trust in the God of Abraham, Isaac, and Jacob. You still have an opportunity to experience life in all its fullness. All you need to do is learn the lessons that the Lord God puts before you and be patient, because change is a process that takes time. You need to find an area of your life where you can be committed to the work for the Lord, which could be becoming a part of your church's community group in a great way. It could be making a commitment to represent Christ at your job or committing to fasting and praying. It could also be committing to study his Word. Your commitment will put you on the right path and help you intersect with the people that will help you get to the next destination of your journey.

If you are someone who is going through or has gone through a divorce, your life has not ended.

It's funny, but I have realized that when God trains someone, he doesn't tell them that he's training them. He didn't tell David that he was in training when a bear came to take his sheep or when a lion took one of his lambs. All David was able to see was the fight that was right in front of him. David didn't see the bear or the lion as a foreshadowing of things to come. That's how it is in our life. We are in training right now. The problem that we are facing requires the gifts that God has given us. When we depend on his word and use our gift, we overcome the problem. That overcoming is the preparation to face the big problem that will propel us to our destiny.

What problems are you facing right now? You have a gift and the word of God contained in the Bible gives you direction and instructions for using that gift. Solve the problems that God puts before you. Don't let being divorced be an excuse for you to sit on the bench. It's time for you to get in the game and show the world that you are well able to conquer the land. Setbacks like divorce are not the final chapter of your life. It's a point in your life where you hit the reset button and start building your life the right way.

I have come to realize that when going through a difficult time in my life, it presents me with the greatest opportunity to show love. I'm talking about real sacrificial love. The type of love that other people will only understand through time. Yes, the setbacks can be embarrassing. It's not easy to face ourselves when we have done wrong; it's not easy to face ourselves when we have made mistakes; or especially when we have made some poor choices. But know this, the Bible says, "...God works all things together for the good of those who love Him, who are called according to his purpose" (Rom. 8.28). Good, bad, or indifferent, if you love the Lord God with all of your heart, all of your mind, all of your soul, and all of your strength and you love your neighbor as you love yourself, all things will work out for your good.

I had dedicated my life to God about 47 years ago and I do not regret one day of it. Not every day has been easy, but God has been with me each and every day. I am a living witness that God does not abandon his children. He has invested a lot in you, and he wants to see his investment mature into a healthy dividend, payout, solution provider to the world. Don't allow a stumbling block to become an impenetrable wall. Trust in the Lord with all your heart. Don't lean on your own understanding. Acknowledge God in all of your ways and he will direct your path.

I had dedicated my life to God about 47 years ago and I do not regret one day of it.

Take away: It's time to hit the reset button and get back on the path that will lead you to success. Be honest with God, others, and yourself about the poor decisions you have made or adverse circumstances that have come upon you. Ask the Lord Jesus to come into your heart and fill you with his wisdom, commitment, drive and love. Jesus said "Ask, and it shall be given you; seek, and ye shall find; knock, and it shall be opened unto you:" (Matt. 7:7).

EPILOGUE

Many of us have gone through some sort of exile. You may be going through it at this very moment. Exile is defined as: "The state of being barred from one's native country". Similar words are expulsion, deportation, banishment, uprooting or eviction. A divorce can feel like exile. Losing a job can feel like exile. Suffering through prolonged illness, surviving the destruction, a valuable relationship or death of a family member or friend, can all feel like some sort of exile. Exile is when you are separated from familiar surroundings; surroundings that make you feel secure. When this is taken away from us, we struggle to make sense of it. We tend to blame others or blame ourselves. We spend valuable time in denial, fear or despair.

Exile is when you are separated from familiar surroundings; surroundings that make you feel secure.

My time in exile has taught me that this alone time can lead to exponential character development. Exile can teach us to face our fears; to do what is right, especially, when it is not easy. However, the most important lesson to learn is to trust what God says, even if it does not make common sense.

There are some great Biblical examples of this. Abram experienced exile when God told him to leave his people and journey to a land without giving advance notice as to where he was going. Basically, God told Abram that he had arrived when he arrived. The pattern was the same. Abram learned to trust in God. When his faith was put to the test, the passing of his tests led to greater character development and a wisdom that only a relationship with the divine can provide. When his time of exile was over, God changed his name from Abram to Abraham; He made him the father of many nations and blessed him with long life, wealth, and influence with God and man.

With Joseph the pattern remained the same. Joseph was exiled from his home when he was sold by his brothers for 20 pieces of silver. He faced many tests. He had the opportunity to take possessions for himself. When he was made the governor of his master's house, he was tempted by his master's wife and thrown in jail for a crime that he did not commit. However, Joseph did not become bitter with God; he served God and served others to the best of his ability. He used his gifts to solve the problems of others. Because of faithfulness to both God and man, he was made Prime Minister of Egypt.

> *Because of faithfulness to both God and man, he was made Prime Minister of Egypt.*

After defeating Goliath, the pattern remained the same for David. David was exiled from the court of

King Saul because King Saul was jealous of David's success. For many years, David was exiled. He suffered hunger, loneliness, and great loss when the enemy captured the wives and children of his army. It got to the point that his soldiers were seriously considering stoning him, but with all that was against him, David trusted in God. He was faithful to do what God commanded him to do. As a result, he recovered all, and he was made King of Judah and Israel.

For our Lord Jesus Christ, the pattern repeats itself. Jesus was exiled from heaven by choice. He left the glory of being a coequal part of the makeup of God, to live and die as a man. The God who needs no food had to depend on his earthly mother, Mary, for milk. In God there is no waste, yet he had to expel waste like every other man. God of the world, who knows all things, had to put his deity aside and learn things just as any other boy would and he had to be taught by the very mankind that he created. What an incredible 33 ½ years of exile. During this time of exile on earth, he earned our unwavering respect and loyalty because he did not commit one sin. Even when provoked, he showed incredible restraint and compassion; above all, he displayed indescribable wisdom. He died on a cruel cross for those of us who love him and those who will never love or respect him, but it was worth it. The Bible says it best, "Looking unto Jesus, the author and finisher of our faith, who for the joy that was set before Him, endured the cross, despising the shame, and is set down at the right hand of the throne of God" (Heb. 12.2).

If you pass your exile experience, the end result is always victory! You will always gain wisdom that will guide you forward and help others along the way. Don't allow your exile experience to stop you. Allow it to shape you into the man or woman that fulfills their God given destiny each and every day.

You may be going through some sort of exile wondering, "How will I get through this?" That is not an appropriate question to ask yourself at this moment. The way out is to do what Christ did when faced with life's most difficult choice. The choice that was made when Jesus was praying so intensely and was under such stress that his sweat became drops of blood, seeing all that he would have to endure to purchase our freedom from a life separated from God. Jesus made up his mind and said, "Nevertheless, not my will but thine be done." (Luk. 22.42).

It's not about finding the right questions to be asking ourselves like, "How did I get here? Who's at fault here? When will this be over?" It took me over five years of saying and living, "Lord, not my will, but let your will be done in my life." He guided my steps and he caused me to meet the right people. One key relationship is all it takes.

It took me over five years of saying and living, "Lord, not my will, but let your will be done in my life."

The day I met Elina, my life took a dramatic turnaround for the better. But that would have never happened if I hadn't surrendered my will, my plans, my perspective, to doing everything God's way. Trust that you were born for such a time as this. The world needs you to help it become a better place. God created you to fit in this world. Seek out his will for your life, not your own agenda. It will lead you to become the best version of you this world has ever seen.

Made in the USA
Columbia, SC
13 October 2021

46669664R00064